W9-BJB-079

Vehicles
On The Move

Deep-diving Submarines

🌱 Crabtree Publishing Company

www.crabtreebooks.com

Created by Bobbie Kalman

Author
Molly Aloian

Editorial director
Kathy Middleton

Project editor
Paul Challen

Editors
Adrianna Morganelli
Crystal Sikkens

Proofreaders
Rachel Stuckey
Janine Belzak

Photo research
Tibor Choleva

Design
Tibor Choleva

Print coordinator
Katherine Berti

Production coordinator
Margaret Amy Salter

Prepress technicians
Margaret Amy Salter
Ken Wright

Consultant
Ron Tarter

Illustrations
All illustrations by Leif Peng

Photographs
Courtesy of Atlantis Submarines International: (page 26 bottom inset, page 27 bottom inset)
Dreamstime.com: © Ericus (pages 6–7); © Convit (page 30 bottom inset)
Photo of press-service of Russian President/www.kremlin.ru (page 29 inset)
© NOAA: Harbor Branch Oceanographic Institution (page 18 top); WHOI, the Alvin Group and the 2004 GOA Seamount Exploration Science Party (page 18 bottom); M. Crosby (page 19 bottom inset); (page 21 bottom right inset)
Science Photo Library: © Sam Ogden (page 31); © Alexis Rosenfeld (page 5)
Shutterstock.com: cover; © Aptyp_koK (page 11 top); © Tim Jenner (page 14 top); © Anna Segeren (pages 18–19); © Stephan Kerkhofs (pages 20–21); © MonkeyBusiness (pages 24–25); Peter Leahy (pages 26–27)
© Ron Tarter (title page)
U.S. Defense Imagery: Don S. Montgomery (page 10 bottom, page 17 top); F. E. Zimmerman (page 11 bottom); (pages 28–29)
U.S. Navy photo by: Paul Farley (table of contents page, page 4); Don S. Montgomery (page 7 inset); Photographer's Mate 2nd Class David C. Duncan (page 9 top); Mass Communication Specialist 1st Class John Parker (page 9 bottom); Mass Communication Specialist 3rd Class Chelsea Kennedy (page 10 top, page 23 top); Mass Communication Specialist 1st Class Scott Taylor (pages 12–13); Photo courtesy of General Dynamics Electric Boat (page 13 bottom); Chief Mass Communication Specialist Marlowe P. Dix (page 14 bottom); Mass Communication Specialist 2nd Class Xander Gamble (page 16 top); MC3 Eric Tretter (pages 16–17); (page 21 left bottom inset); Mass Communication Specialist 3rd Class Spencer Mickler (page 22); Mass Communication Specialist 2nd Class Barry Hirayama (page 23 bottom); Mass Communication Specialist 1st Class Tiffini M. Jones (page 24 bottom); Chief Mass Communication Specialist Shawn P. Eklund (page 25 top); Chief Yeoman Alphonso Braggs (page 25 bottom) –All Released

---

Library and Archives Canada Cataloguing in Publication

Aloian, Molly
Deep-diving submarines / Molly Aloian.

(Vehicles on the move)
Includes index.
Issued also in electronic format.
ISBN 978-0-7787-2728-6 (bound).--ISBN 978-0-7787-2735-4 (pbk.)

1. Submarines (Ships)--Juvenile literature. I. Title. II. Series:
Vehicles on the move

VM365.A46 2011   j623.825'7   C2011-900166-7

Library of Congress Cataloging-in-Publication Data

Aloian, Molly.
Deep-diving submarines / Molly Aloian.
p. cm. -- (Vehicles on the move)
Includes index.
ISBN 978-0-7787-2735-4 (pbk. : alk. paper) -- ISBN 978-0-7787-2728-6 (reinforced library binding : alk. paper) -- ISBN 978-1-4271-9697-2 (electronic (pdf))
1. Submarines (Ships)--Juvenile literature. 2. Deep diving--Juvenile literature. I. Title. II. Series.

VM365.A46 2011
623.82'7--dc22

2010052611

Crabtree Publishing Company

www.crabtreebooks.com   1-800-387-7650

Printed in the U.S.A./022011/CJ20101228

Published in Canada
Crabtree Publishing
616 Welland Ave.
St. Catharines, ON
L2M 5V6

Published in the United States
Crabtree Publishing
PMB 59051
350 Fifth Avenue, 59th Floor
New York, New York 10118

Published in the United Kingdom
Crabtree Publishing
Maritime House
Basin Road North, Hove
BN41 1WR

Published in Australia
Crabtree Publishing
386 Mt. Alexander Rd.
Ascot Vale (Melbourne)
VIC 3032

Contents

Down below

A submarine is a boat that travels underwater. It can even move under thick layers of ice. A submarine is quiet and hard to see below the water's surface. The fastest submarines can reach a speed of about 47 miles per hour (75.6 km per hour) when moving underwater.

Most military submarines, like the USS Dallas *shown above, have long, tube-shaped bodies.*

Subs at work

Submarines can do many jobs. Research submarines explore different parts of the world's oceans. Military submarines are used in warfare. Small submarines can travel more than 30,000 feet (9,144 m) below the surface of the water.

Research submarine Nautile *is retrieved by its support ship. It is used to explore the ocean floors and collect samples.* Nautile *can dive to a depth of 19,685 feet (6,000 meters).*

Take a closer look

Submarines can do jobs that no other boats can. Submarines are made up of many parts. Each part does a different job. This submarine is a military submarine.

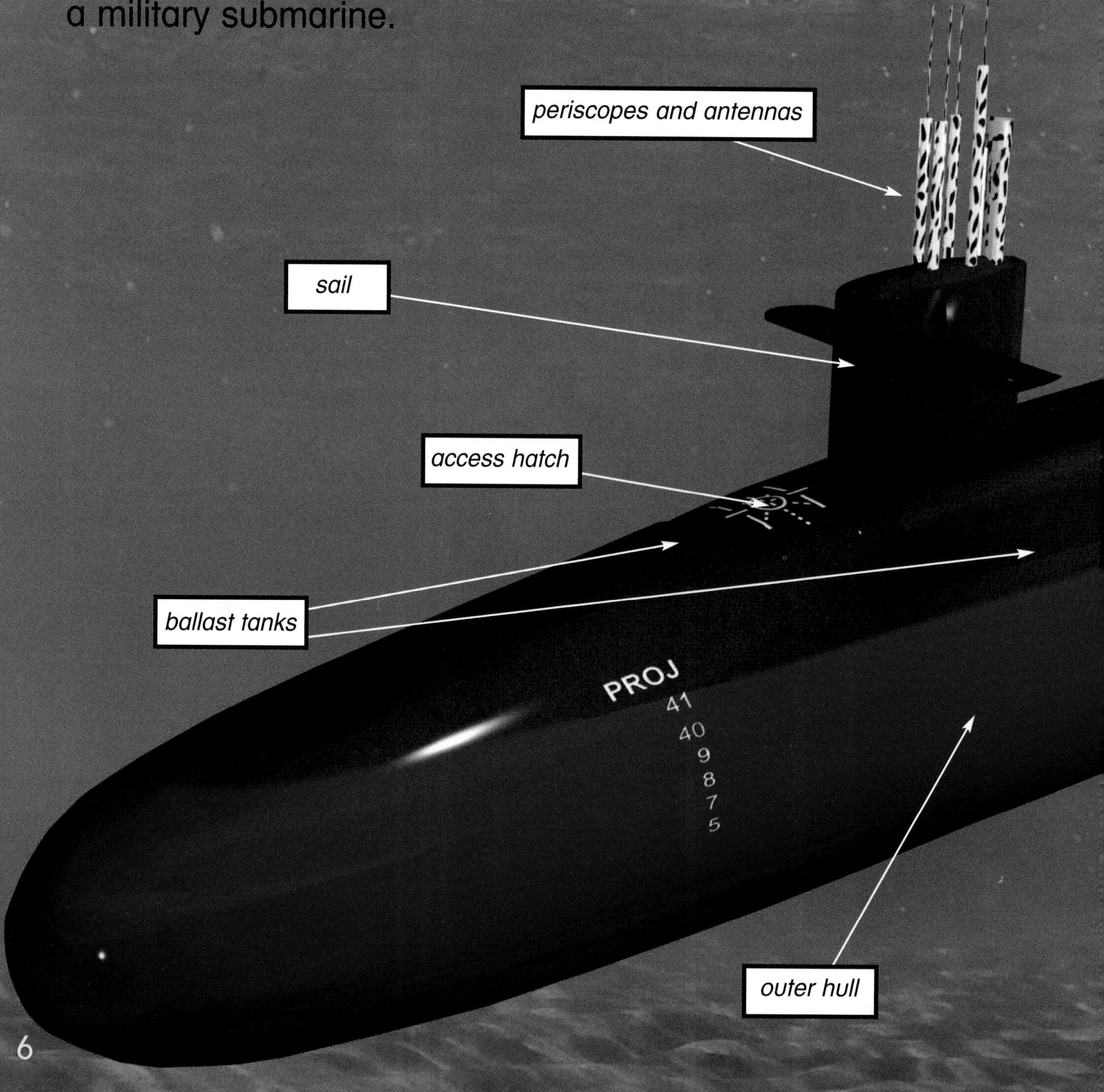

periscopes and antennas

sail

access hatch

ballast tanks

PROJ
41
40
9
8
7
5

outer hull

The **hull** is the largest part of the submarine. There is an inner hull and an outer hull. Crew members work, eat, and sleep inside the inner hull. **Ballast tanks** fill with water and force the submarine underwater. The sail controls the submarine when it is on the surface of the water. The propeller moves the submarine forward or backward. A submarine has an engine. The engine gives the submarine power. Power makes the submarine move.

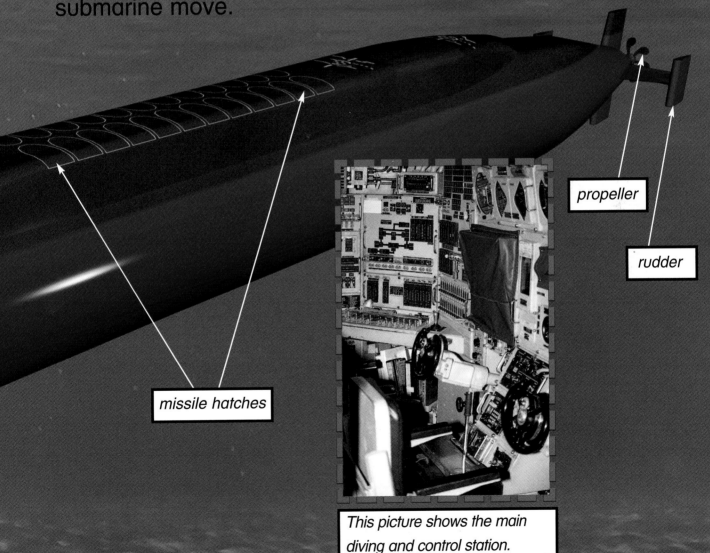

propeller

rudder

missile hatches

This picture shows the main diving and control station.

Diving deep

To go underwater, a submarine's ballast tanks must be filled with water. This makes the submarine heavier so it can move downward. To rise to the surface, a submarine empties the water from its ballast tanks. Powerful air pumps force the water out of the tanks.

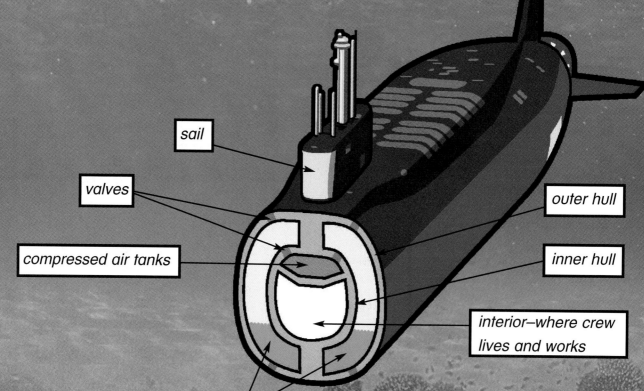

sail

valves

compressed air tanks

outer hull

inner hull

interior—where crew lives and works

ballast tanks—partly filled with water

Air is lighter than water

With air inside the ballast tanks, the submarine is lighter and can rise to the surface of the water. Air is lighter than water. Filling and emptying the ballast tanks allows the submarine to rise or sink in the water as quickly or slowly as necessary.

If necessary, a submarine can surface at high speeds. If it rises too quickly, a submarine can leap out of the water into the air.

The guided-missile submarine USS Georgia begins to submerge. The ballast tanks become flooded with water and the air inside the tanks is released out of the submarine.

The periscope

A submarine has a **periscope**. A periscope is a tube that sticks up out of the water. It has a mirror or TV system that shows the captain the view above the surface of the water. The periscope has an eyepiece for the captain to look through.

This boy is looking through the periscope while on a public tour.

Cased in

The periscope has a thick, hard, waterproof case. The case protects the periscope from getting wet. When not in use, a submarine's periscope is pulled into the hull. Military submarines sometimes have two periscopes.

periscope view

antenna

periscopes

To use a periscope, submarines need to be close to the surface. This is called periscope depth or PD.

Nuclear power

Some submarines run on nuclear power. Nuclear power is produced from powerful nuclear reactions. Nuclear power heats up water, creating a lot of steam. The pressure of the steam turns the submarine's propeller.

The Los Angeles class are nuclear-powered fast attack submarines in the U.S. Navy.

Long gone

Nuclear submarines can travel underwater for long periods of time. They do not need to stop for fuel so they can stay underwater for months at a time. They are the biggest and most expensive machines under the sea!

This submarine is 453 feet (138 m) long.

Research submarines

Some submarines are designed to explore the ocean floor. They search for species of deep-ocean fish and gigantic crabs. They also search for sunken ships and lost treasures, such as valuable gold coins.

Research submarines have robotic arms attached to their hulls. The "claws" can pick up samples of rocks on the ocean floor and bring them to the surface.

The Johnson-Sea-Link *research submersible explores the ocean floor.*

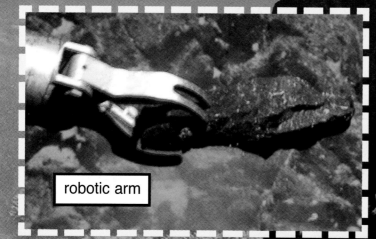

robotic arm

Smaller submersible

A **submersible** is a small research submarine that can dive deep into the ocean. It can explore places that are too small for large submarines to get to. A submersible called *Alvin* found the remains of the the sunken ship the *Titanic* in 1985.

Alvin *is famous in the submersible world.*

Keeping track

Some research submarines are used to make sure the oceans stay healthy and clean. Researchers on these submarines keep track of pollution and overfishing in the oceans. They also check for oil leaks and chemical spills from ships. Keeping track of marine life is also important.

Unlike military submarines, research submarines have windows called viewports on their hulls.

ROVs

Researchers sometimes use **remote-operated vehicles** or ROVs. A person on a ship or a submersible sits in front of a television screen and controls the ROV's underwater movements with a special joystick. Strong lights help the operator see the ocean floor. The person can control the ROV's robotic arms and hands.

The remote-operated vehicle, Super Scorpio, *is loaded aboard a support ship.*

Rescuing submarines

If a submarine starts to leak, has engine trouble, or other problems, it will need to send a call to a **rescue submarine**. A rescue submarine is called a deep submergence rescue vehicle or DSRV. These submarines rescue crew members and trapped submarines.

In an emergency, a submarine rescue chamber is lowered to the damaged submarine and locked to the escape hatch.

Locked on

A DSRV can go down about 3,500 feet (1,067 m). When underwater, the DSRV can lock onto the hatch of the submarine in trouble with a special watertight lock. A small number of crew members evacuate at one time and the DSRV carries them to safety. Some submarines have 100 or more crew members, so a rescue mission could take several hours and many trips of the DSRV.

Divers in special deep-dive suits can be lowered to a depth of 2,000 feet (610 m).

If a sick or injured person is being rescued, a small boat or helicopter transfers the patient to a surface ship with doctors onboard.

Under the ice

Nuclear submarines can stay underwater for months at a time. Because they do not need to refuel, they can travel for long periods under the polar ice. When they are ready to surface, the submarines can break through the ice in places where the ice is not very thick.

Crew members onboard this submarine were under the ice for weeks. They are glad to get out for a stroll in the stark beauty of the Arctic wilderness.

Thin ice

Scientists can travel onboard nuclear submarines to monitor the effects of global warming on the polar ice cap. They measure the thickness of the underwater ice. The ice pack at the North Pole has become smaller in recent years. In the summer the Arctic ice can be as thin as six feet (1.8 m).

A submarine is shown here surfacing through the polar ice of the Arctic.

Polar bears can be very curious. These three approached the fast attack submarine USS Honolulu *while it was surfaced 280 miles (450 km) from the North Pole. The bears investigated the "intruder" for almost two hours before leaving.*

25

Tourist submarines

Tourist submarines take people
on underwater tours of the oceans.
These submarines have special
windows through which people
can see ocean animals and
coral reefs up close.

Tourist submarines offer undersea adventure trips.

All aboard!

Tourist submarines are actually submersibles because they are usually battery-powered. The biggest ones can carry approximately 60 passengers and can travel down about 150 feet (46 m). There are about 50 tourist submarines in the world today.

The biggest submarine

Russia makes some of the biggest submarines in the world. They are called Typhoon-class submarines. A Typhoon is a military submarine that is about 560 feet (170 m) long. They are nuclear-powered submarines. Typhoon-class submarines are fast and very quiet.

A Typhoon-class submarine can travel at about 29 mph (47 km/h). It can dive 400 feet (122 m) below the surface of the water.

Taking a dip

A Typhoon-class submarine can stay underwater for almost 120 days at a time and can carry 150 crew members. This submarine has comfortable lounge seats and special lighting for the crew members. It even has a swimming pool!

The Borei-class is the newest class of nuclear-powered Russian Navy submarines. Borei-class submarines are bigger and will replace the Typhoon-class now in service.

Into the future

The submarines of the future will be faster and quieter. The U.S. Navy is working on building submarines that are more powerful and that can dive deeper. Luxury submarines for tourists will also be larger and be able to dive deeper.

Swimming like a fish

The U.S. Navy is researching the use of artificial muscles instead of propellers. This will let the submarines move through the water like a fish, using fins for steering. These submarines will also be able to pick up even the slightest movements or vibrations underwater.

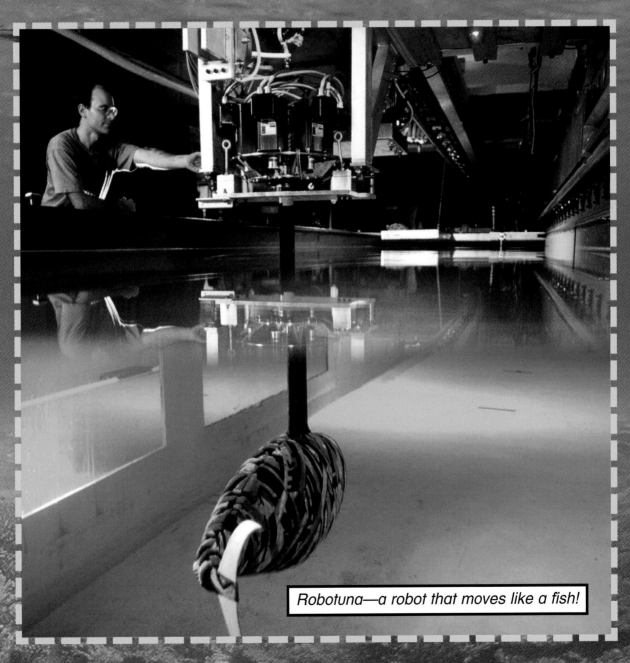

Robotuna—a robot that moves like a fish!

Words to know and Index

ballast tanks
pages 6, 7, 8–9

remote-operated vehicles
page 21

submersible
pages 18–19, 21, 27

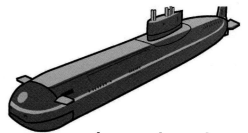

nuclear submarine
pages 12–13, 14, 24, 25, 28–29

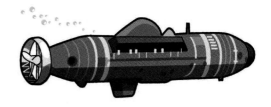

rescue submarine
pages 5, 22–23

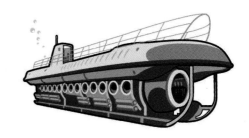

tourist submarine
pages 26–27, 30

Other index words